upcycled JEWELRY

BAGS, BELTS, and more

35 beautiful projects
made from recycled materials

Linda Peterson

CICO BOOKS
LONDON NEW YORK

For my husband, Dana, who's always been my biggest cheerleader. I'm so glad we're soulmates. I love you!

Published in 2014 by CICO Books
An imprint of Ryland Peters & Small
519 Broadway, 5th Floor, New York NY 10012
20–21 Jockey's Fields, London WC1R 4BW
www.rylandpeters.com

10 9 8 7 6 5 4 3 2 1

A CIP catalog record for this book is available from
the Library of Congress and the British Library.

ISBN: 978-1-78249-151-4

Printed in China

Project Editor: Marie Clayton
Designer: Isobel Gillan
Step Photography: Geoff Dann
Style Photography: Emma Mitchell
Stylist: Luis Peral-Aranda
Template Illustration: Stephen Dew

In-House Editor: Carmel Edmonds
Publishing Manager: Penny Craig
Art Director: Sally Powell
Production Controller: Meskerem Berhane
Publisher: Cindy Richards

contents

introduction

My family jokes with me that they have to ask first before they throw anything away. They know of my rat-packing ways and how I love to keep stuff. Sometimes it's memorable stuff and sometimes, well, I admit, it's garbage stuff—but *good* garbage stuff! If you've read my other books, such as *Art+Life* or *Creative Ideas to Organize Your Home*, you likely know that I am a self-proclaimed, dumpster diving diva. So, that's no new news. But, if you're not familiar with my style, I can just see that picture forming in your mind of me literally jumping into random trash dumpsters, feet in the air as I dive down to the darkest dumpster depths and begin sifting through loads of garbage looking for plastic bottles, flinging cans and other miscellaneous objects into the air and coming out covered in… well, we just won't go there. No, no, that's not at all what I mean, although maybe that's not too far fetched? On several occasions I have been seen—and even photographed with shovel in one hand and glorious "treasure" in the other—as I visit the "treasure ditch" on our family farm that no one has touched in over 30 years.

It's a challenge to repurpose and one I take on with great passion: to give old discarded things, or newly discarded things, a new and purposeful life and keep them out of the landfill. There is a mystery and a buried story that lies deep inside discarded items. It's almost as if they cry out, wanting their story told. I find that particularly fascinating—it really starts my creative imagination.

The trend of upcycling and recycling is gaining much popularity with indie crafters and I believe it will only continue to gain

I'm even taking this book a step further, because I've created a play list on my YouTube channel especially for you, containing how-to video tutorials featuring some of the techniques I've used here. While a book with step-by-step photos is great, sometimes you just need to see the action. So now you'll have it all: pictures, written instructions, and a video to enhance your creating experience. Along with that, I'll have a special Pinterest board with links to those specific videos and other helpful resources to make sure that you're inspired to create these projects and that you are successful throughout the process. All you need to do is follow me on Pinterest and look for the *Upcycled Jewelry, Belts, Bags, and More* board for all the links to the YouTube videos, and check me out on my YouTube channel. You'll find all of the information for Pinterest and YouTube in the resource section just below my name.

strength. More and more artisans and designers are finding ways to earn income by catering to niche markets of people wanting to purchase handmade. You name it—they will make it! And why not use recycled materials? They cost next to free and they're pretty easily found. Seems to me like a no-brainer.

If you're new to this idea, or even new to creating something, you may think you have little to work with in terms of materials and tools. It's no fun to get all excited about creating something only to find out that you have to have loads of expensive tools, spend a lot of time looking for the materials, and have no time left over to even begin making the project. I get it! That's why my books always feature projects with materials that are easy to find and create with equipment that you probably already have. You may have to purchase a tool or two, but consider that a gift to yourself that you really deserve—and will use again and again on future projects.

reduce, reuse, upcycle!

There is a definite difference between recycling and upcycling. Recycling takes consumable materials and breaks them down so that their base materials can be used to make new product—much of the time this results in a lesser quality product. Upcycling, however, does not break down these materials: it uses them as they are to make another item, making it the same quality if not better than the original.

There was a time when upcycling wasn't cool, it was a necessity. During the 1930s and 40s, families had very limited resources and were forced to reuse and repurpose what they could. They used items over and over again until they were no longer useful. So it's not really a new concept. Now though, upcycling is cool! You'll be cool if you upcycle

and we want to be cool, right? The old saying "What was old, will become new" is never truer than in this case. While some still upcycle because of necessity, others find it trendy and enjoy the challenge of using upcycled materials to rival designs found in high end department stores.

I think it goes without saying that we all want the best for our environment. Recycling, while it has a somewhat positive influence on our environment, still requires machinery and energy to break down the materials into something reusable. Upcycling only requires personal energy, imagination, and some simple elbow grease! By repurposing our "trash" we are not only saving it from an ugly death in a landfill, we are giving it a new purpose and a new life and we are rewarded by saving energy and money.

I've kept the focus of this book on some of my favorite recycling materials, such as plastics, metals, and inner tubes because of their versatility and ease to acquire and work with. But don't just limit yourself to these or even to these projects. Allow this book to kick start your creativity when it comes to things you might otherwise discard. Can an old sweater be repurposed into a pillow, the sleeves into pouches for our electronic mobile devices? Or use denim from jeans to create a handbag—you get the idea….

Let your neighbors know what kinds of things you are after, call up the bicycle shops and the tire shops in your area and ask them to save you old inner tubes. Get to know the servers at your favorite restaurant because they may have loads of cans and soda tabs at their disposal. Yes, I've even been known to ask the flight attendants on airplanes, because guess what all the drinks are served in? Cans! And cans have tabs and interesting designs. Turn it into a treasure hunt—make it fun.

So now, go—go through your trash, your closets, thrift stores and find all those things you can upcycle. Make friends with the people at bike shops, tire shops, restaurants, since they will be more than glad to get rid of the items you are after. Make a positive impact on the environment, dignify your trash, and make a fashion statement too!

TOOLS, materials, and TECHNIQUES

It's always much easier—and more fun—to make things if you have the correct tools. There are loads of specialized jewelry tools available, but I've selected these basic tools because they are must-haves and will give you lots of value for your money. This section also covers techniques that I use over and over again on several projects. A few additional tips can be found in the individual projects themselves.

TOOLS

Many of these tools can be found in hardware and local craft stores. There are also many resources on the internet.

Basic tools

These are the tools that I've used in nearly every project in the book. Before going out to purchase, have a look around because you most likely have many of them already.

Metal shears: Specialized shears to cut metal such as aluminum cans.

Standard wire cutters: Useful for creating wire bails, making jump rings, and snipping off excess amounts of wire.

Standard hammer: Used to flatten and to set rivets, grommets, and snaps

Standard pliers: Used to grip pieces and hold small pieces in place away from your fingers.

Crimping pliers: Used to squeeze crimping beads and tubes onto beading wire.

Concave bending pliers: Allow you to easily bend wire when forming it into rounded shapes to create loops for wire wrapping or bail making. If you can't find concave bending pliers, you could use round-nose pliers instead.

Duckbill scissors: I use these to cut open bicycle inner tubes because I find the large flat blade holds the rubber in place allowing me to create a straighter cut. They are also useful in cutting metal.

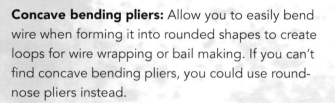

Standard scissors: Make sure you have a nice sharp pair so that you can cut through the materials in this book easily.

Setting tools

These tools are necessary in setting various rivets, eyelets, and grommets. Make sure you have the right size setter to match the size of the rivet or eyelet you are using.

Grommet setter: This is similar to an eyelet setter but is larger. It includes an anvil that the grommet sits down into ready for setting.

Eyelet setter: Eyelet setters tend to be smaller than grommet setters or rivet setters.

Rivet setter: Used in this book to set double-sided rivets. The rivet fits into a same-size recess in the anvil so it remains curved when set with a hammer.

Cone rivet setter: The head on this setter is a cone rather than a rounded tip. This type of setter flares the rivet into a star shape on the back when set.

Bench block: A hard surface used in conjunction with setting eyelets, grommets, and rivets.

Cutting and dismantling tools

I use a variety of punches specifically for leather to create the appropriate size holes for the size of eyelet or rivet I am working with. These can be found in craft stores or in specialty leather stores. They often come in sets with a variety of sizes, which offer good value for the money.

Bike chain tool: Used to remove links from bike chains.

Circle leather punches: These create holes for eyelets, grommets, and rivets. I use a variety of sizes to create decorative patterns. Some have interchangeable nibs.

Dremel cutter: (round disk) This sawing disk is especially made to cut through metal. A variety of different Dremel attachments can be found in hardware stores.

Dremel and drill bit: Used to create holes for jewelry.

Hand punch: This creates small holes for jump rings in jewelry. Hand punches are used for materials that are lightweight and soft.

Heating and stamping tools

In this book, these tools are used for forming and decorating plastic.

Lighter tool: (right center) Useful when you need to have more control as you are heating plastic and forming it into shapes.

Heat gun: (below right) Also used to heat plastic. Use this tool when you want to shrink the plastic to a smaller size. Since the heat is not as focused, this tool tends to take a little while longer than when using a direct heat source, such as the lighter.

Protective Teflon gloves: (below) Protect your hands from heat as well as from sharp metal edges when cutting.

Rubber stamps: (top right) These come either mounted or unmounted and are used to stamp impressions into plastic.

SAFETY TIP

I wear Teflon coated gloves whenever I work on material with sharp edges, such as metal from soda cans. Make sure they fit well so that you can easily maneuver your materials in them and prevent injury.

MATERIALS

The materials covered here are all the main ones used in the projects, but also see page 10 for ideas on finding and upcycling materials.

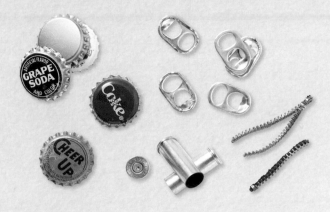

Recycled metal

Look for suitable metals to be up cycled, such as bottle tops, soda can tabs, spent bullet casings, and zipper teeth. I keep the small items in jars.

Plastics

Many different types of plastic can easily be upcycled into jewelry, including chip/crisp packets, straws, gift cards, CD spacers, and plastic bottles. I keep a large plastic tub of these types of plastics bottles and containers of various colors in my studio. When the tub gets full, I send the extra off to the recycle center, that way my collecting doesn't get out of control. For plastics that shrink the best, look for the #5 and #6 in the triangle. Most food grade plastics are #1—some of these are suitable and some are not. Do some experimenting as it seems that the process of creating the plastic shapes can vary the way they shrink and melt once heated.

Inner tube rubber

Make friends with your local bike shop. They often have old inner tubes around that they would love to have you take off their hands. If you prefer, you can purchase new ones quite inexpensively. The ones I used the most for the projects in this book are a standard 27 in. bicycle inner tubes. You can also use an inner tube from a car or truck, but these tend to be thicker and harder to sew in your machine. They also lack the interesting textures so I find the bicycle tubes easier and more desirable to work with.

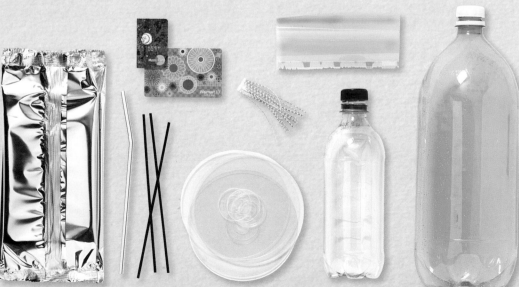

Belt buckles

These are available in a range of sizes and designs. I keep an eye out for interesting belt buckles whenever I shop at thrift stores and garage sales. You can also purchase new ones at leather shops and craft stores.

Metal

Metal from soda and drink cans is thinner and can be easily cut and you'll find cans with loads of interesting designs. Remove the ends of the can and keep only the flat metal—this helps to save space and allows you the room to collect more.

Old license plates and similar decorative metal pieces can often be found at yard sales or on eBay.

Beads

This is a very small selection of the thousands of beads and spacer beads that are available. For this book, I use quite a few 2 mm round spacer beads and flat roundel beads. I buy these in bulk and find that they are very versatile, so I use them constantly when creating jewelry. I also take apart old jewelry and reclaim the beads from necklaces, bracelets, and earrings.

Chains and stringing

Chains are available in different weights and metals but also in different designs, so you can choose the best one to suit your project. Necklaces can also be made using ribbon or cord.

Sewing materials

Some of the projects use simple sewing techniques but we also use zippers and buttons as decorative elements. Reclaim these from used clothing.

Wires

I mainly use 24-gauge or 22-gauge wire in these projects, which is available in different metal finishes and in assorted colors. The thinner wire is useful for wrapping and making loops, while the heavier wire is used for strength and durability.

Findings

A finding is the term used to describe all the small components that are used to join, fasten, or assemble jewelry pieces.

Bezels blanks are designed to have a decorative stone or gem set in the center, they can also be filled with paper designs and resin. These are great for focal pieces in your jewelry.

Earring wires (top left) are ideal to make earrings, and **ring blanks** (center) for rings. Headpins and **eye pins** (bottom left) can be used to make dangles (see page 25). **Earring hoops** (right) are ideal if you want to make more dramatic earrings.

There are many different fasteners available so you can choose something to suit your project. **Crimp rings** (top left) are used to fasten wires or thread onto a **jump ring** (bottom left) or ring of a clasp. **Cord ends** (center top) are used in the same way on rounded leather or fabric cords, while decorative **ribbon ends** (top right) are useful for flat materials. **Lobster clasps** (bottom center) can hook onto any plain or decorative **end ring** (middle).

Grommets, **eyelets**, and **snaps** come in many sizes and different color metals. They can be used both as decorative elements and as part of a fastening solution.

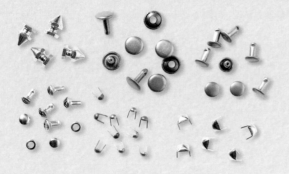

There are also many different types and styles of **rivets** available, some designed to be fairly unobtrusive and others as more of a statement. Again, they can be used to fasten two pieces together or as a decorative element.

Connectors are used to join two pieces together, such as when adding a handle to a bag or joining two ends of a belt. Here we show examples of a **swivel trigger snap** (left), **swivel D-rings** (center), and a **decorative hasp** (right).

These are just a few examples of the thousands of **decorative findings** that are available.

D-rings are used at the end of belts and straps—you can fold the end of a strap over the flat bar of the D-ring and then use it as a base to attach the strap. Split rings are mainly used for making key fobs.

Conchos are purely decorative pieces that are fixed on with a small screw from the reverse.

Adhesives

There are several types of adhesive and it's important to choose the correct one for the material and the project. The clear caulk is used to enable paint to cling to rubber. Silicon-based adhesive is used for most of the projects but there are special adhesives for vinyl, fabric, and plastic. Fray stop is used to prevent fabric from fraying and tacky glue is a multi-purpose adhesive. Masking tape is low-tack so it can be removed without damaging the surface, so it is useful for holding items temporarily or as a base for marking. Double-stick sheet has adhesive on both sides, so can be used to join layers together. Black electrical tape is used in some projects to give added strength to seams.

Coloring materials

Nail varnish, alcohol inks, paint, paint pen—these are various materials that are used to give extra color and interest to clear or silver metal materials. Nail varnish is a good choice on metal because it clings to the surface better than acrylic paint. Alcohol inks are transparent so you can see the material underneath through the color. Paint pens allow you to draw designs and patterns easily.

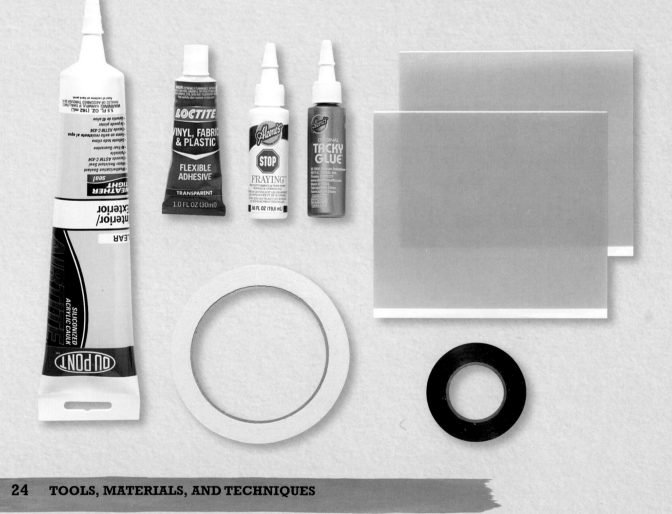

TECHNIQUES

You will use the techniques in this section several times in different projects; a cross-reference in the project will bring you to the correct page in the techniques section. Any special techniques that are specific to a particular project are detailed within that project.

creating a beaded dangle

1 Thread the chosen bead or beads and spacer beads onto a headpin.

2 Use concave bending pliers to curve the top of the headpin into a loop, centering the loop over the beads. Cut off the excess headpin.

opening and closing jump rings

Use this simple method to open and close jump rings so you can use them to attach items together.

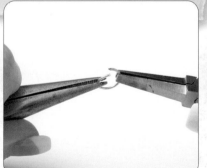

1 To open the jump ring, hold a pair of pliers on each side of the join and twist the pliers slightly in opposite directions to open up a gap.

2 To close the ring, repeat the twisting action in reverse to bring the two ends back together neatly.

HELPFUL HINT

It's not a good idea to open a jump ring by pulling the ends apart—this will distort the shape and it will be very hard to get it back into a perfect circle. Open them as shown here and they will stay perfectly round.

melting plastic

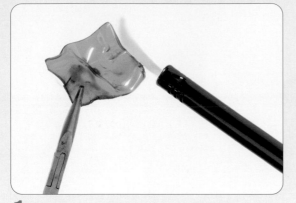

1 Use a lighter to gently melt pieces of plastic to give them curved edges and uneven shapes. You only need the heat source near to the plastic, there is no need to hold it in the flame.

HELPFUL HINT

Wear protective gloves when cutting cans open to avoid being cut by any sharp metal edges.

cutting cans

1 Make a slot with the craft knife near the top edge of the can.

2 Slide the blade of the scissors inside the slot and cut around to remove the top of the can. Remove the bottom end the same way.

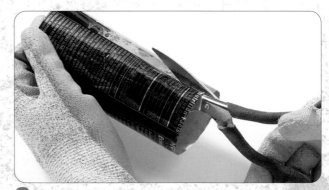

3 Cut down the can at a suitable point and then carefully open it out flat.

using a crimp bead

A crimp bead is usually used to attach a jump ring or other finding to the end of a length of bead stringing material, but can also be used to hold beads in place along a length of filament.

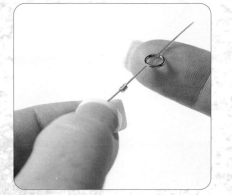

1 String a crimp bead onto the bead stringing wire or filament and then add a jump ring.

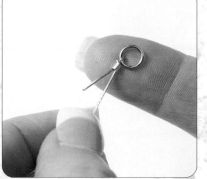

2 Fold the wire or filament over the jump ring and back through the crimp bead. Pull the loop tight against the jump ring.

3 Using crimping pliers, squeeze the crimp bead down firmly against the beading wire.

4 If you are using the crimp bead at the end of the wire, trim the end of the wire back to approximately ½ in. (12 mm), but no less than ¼ in. (6 mm) to prevent the end pulling back through the crimp bead.

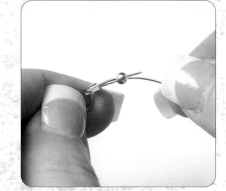

5 At the end, string the first few beads over the end of the wire also, to conceal it. If you are using the crimp bead to hold a bead or other piece in place on a length of filament, just add a crimp bead on either side in the same way.

soda tab crochet

This uses a very simple and basic crochet stitch so it is very easy to learn. You just have to remember to crochet with the tabs facing each other and only open them out into a flat fabric at the end of the row.

1 Using the crochet thread off the reel, make a slip knot as shown. Place the slip knot on the crochet hook. Hold the hook in your right hand and keep the thread under tension with the fingers of your left hand.

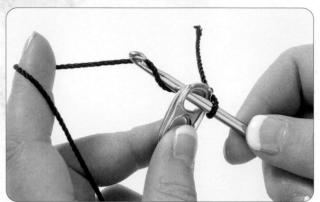

2 Place two soda tabs (right sides together) on top of one another, holding them with finger and thumb of your left hand. Put the crochet hook through the right-hand hole in both tabs and catch the thread behind.

3 Pull the thread through so you now have two loops on your hook—the original slip knot and the new loop. Put the crochet hook over the top of both tabs and catch the thread behind. Pull the thread through both loops on the hook, so you now have one loop on the hook. You have now completed one single (UK double) crochet stitch. Make a second stitch through the same hole of the tabs.

4 To continue the row, add two more tabs, one at the front and one at the back, aligning the right-hand hole over the left-hand hole of the previous two tabs and with the flat sides of both facing each other as before. Make two stitches through the aligned hole of all four tabs. Repeat this step until you have the number of tabs you need.

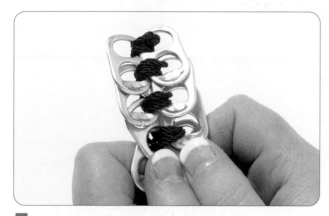

5 Open out the two rows just made so the flat sides are both facing up. You can add more rows by placing the next tab on top of the end tab of one of these rows and following steps 2–4.

6 To finish off at the end of each row, cut a long end of yarn and thread it into a yarn needle. Weave the yarn end through several stitches on the reverse and then trim off the end neatly.

making holes and setting

Holes can either be used as a decorative feature or made as the first step of setting an eyelet, grommet, or rivet. You will need a softer surface to hammer into—I've used a plastic block or you can substitute a block of wood. Do not use a steel bench block or you will damage your leather punches.

1 Mark the position of all the holes clearly on the material. Place the material on a plastic block and then punch each hole out with a suitable size leather hole punch.

2 If you want to add an eyelet to the hole, place the setting tool on the bench block and place the top half of the eyelet on top with the ridged side facing upward.

3 Thread one of the holes in the material onto the eyelet.

4 Place the other half of the setting tool on top and hammer down firmly, which spreads the ridge of the eyelet out into a ring to seal the edges of the hole.

5 To add a double-sided rivet to a hole, thread the peg of a rivet up through the hole—which can be one you have just punched into any material or a hole in a metal piece, such as a bicycle chain link.

6 Add a second link onto the peg—or any other piece that you want to rivet in place—and then place the cap half of the rivet on top.

7 Place the rivet on a bench block and place the rivet setter on top. Hammer down firmly to seal the cap to the rivet.

removing chain links

1 Insert the end link of the chain in the chain link tool with the pin aligned with the end of the screw.

2 Screw the tool down until the pin is pushed out completely and the last link comes free.

HELPFUL HINT
- - - - - - - - - - - - - - - - - - - -
Clean used bicycle chains by scrubbing them well with hot water and detergent to remove all the grease and grime.

Chapter ONE

simple
and CHIC

Oh, the hunt for buried treasure—and it begins with you!
I invite you to treasure hunt for all the materials that you have
in your home that can be upcycled and given a new purpose.
This chapter will get you thinking creatively and out of the
box, so to speak. You'll find the designs simple, easy to make,
and so chic to wear!

razzle-dazzle tassel earrings

One of my favorite recycled materials to work with is bicycle inner tube. The faceted and silver beads add a touch of sparkle to these funky black tassel earrings, which look as if they are made of expensive leather. This is a great project to make with all the left over bits and pieces of tube from other projects.

YOU WILL NEED

Basic tools

Small piece of bicycle inner tube

2 eye pins with large eyes

24-gauge silver wire

8 size 2 mm silver beads

4 small black crystal faceted beads

Pair of fishhook earring wires

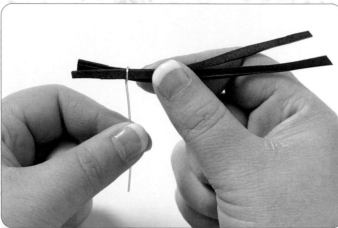

1 Cut 4 strips of rubber about 1⁄16 in. (1.5 mm) wide and about 3 in. (7.5 cm) long. Thread two strips through the loop of the eye pin.

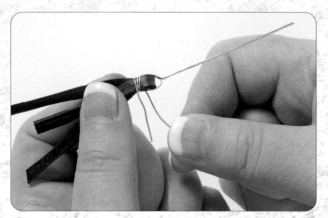

2 Using a short length of the silver wire, wrap tightly around the rubber strips just below the eye of the eye pin. Trim to uneven lengths.

3 Cut six small squares of rubber. Thread the following onto the eye pin in this order: silver bead, faceted bead, rubber square, silver bead, rubber square, silver bead, rubber square, faceted bead, silver bead.

HELPFUL HINT

If you can't find an eye pin with a large enough eye, make your own from a length of 22-gauge silver wire by creating a loop at the end with concave bending pliers.

4 Create a loop in the other end of the eye pin with concave bending pliers. Attach the earring wire and close the loop. Repeat all steps for the second earring.

bike-chain pendant

This is a really quick and easy project to make. The industrial look of the bicycle chain links contrasts with the more feminine feel of the black pearl bead dangle, making it a nice conversation piece.

YOU WILL NEED

Basic tools

2 bicycle chain repair links

24-gauge silver wire

1 headpin

2 mm spacer bead

Black pearl bead

Ball chain with clasp

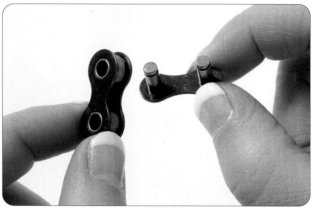

1 You should have two sets of links: one set has holes and the other has double pins. Place one link with holes over one of the pin links.

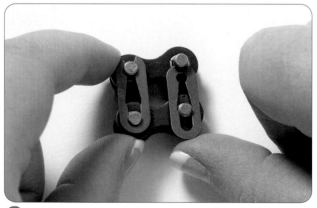

2 Add the second link onto the other side of the double pin. Position the links as shown in the picture and insert another double pin through the two remaining holes.

3 Secure the pin links with the clips as shown, by placing the widest section of the clip over the pin link and sliding it forward into place.

4 Cut a length of silver wire and thread one end around a post of one of the links. Using pliers, wrap the end of the wire around to secure into place and trim off excess wire.

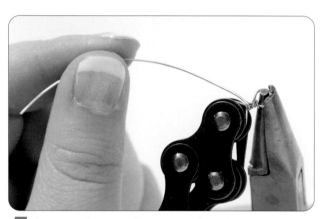

5 Create a loop with concave bending pliers and wrap the end of the wire around the base of the loop. Snip off excess wire. Repeat steps 4–5 on the opposite end of the pendant.

HELPFUL HINTS

It's easier and quicker to use single repair links for this project as I have done, rather than removing a link from a bicycle chain.

Use any chain of your choice for this pendant but make sure the wire loop you make is big enough to thread it through.

6 Make a bead dangle as described on page 25 and thread it onto one of the loops. Close the loop with pliers. Thread the chain through the loop at the top and close the clasp.

sea glass earrings

These pretty dangly pieces look rather like pieces of sea-worn glass, but they are much lighter plastic. Use any design you like for the stamp and you can color them to match a favorite outfit.

YOU WILL NEED

Basic tools

Plastic CD spacer

Sanding block

Heat gun

Rubber stamp

Acrylic paint in color of choice

Paintbrush

Paper towel

Antiquing medium

24-gauge wire

2 decorative link rings approximately ½ in. (12 mm) in diameter or size desired

2 small beads

Pair of earring wires

1 Hold the plastic disc in one hand and break off random shapes using pliers. Arrange the shapes and decide which ones you want to use—you need two pairs of roughly equal sizes and shapes.

2 Carefully sand all round each piece to smooth off any sharp edges or corners.

3 Hold a piece with the pliers and gently heat it with a heat gun, which will cause it to shrink and soften.

4 Using an ordinary rubber stamp, immediately press the stamp into the surface of the plastic while it is still soft. Repeat with the other pieces.

5 Drill a hole into the top of each piece.

6 Paint over the top of each piece—since the plastic is clear there is no need to paint the back unless you want to.

7 Use a paper towel to apply a small amount of antiquing medium. I like to leave some of the medium inside the cracks to highlight the texture.

HELPFUL HINTS

The CD spacer is the clear plastic insert often found at the top and bottom of packs of CDs and DVDs to protect the discs.

Hang the plastic pieces at different heights by adjusting the length of the wire before beginning to wrap.

I also like to experiment with different stamp patterns and colors—I chose a Pool Blue for my earrings. You can achieve a variety of looks with this one simple technique.

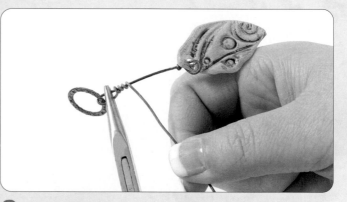

8 Cut a length of wire about 4 in. (10 cm) long and loop one end through one of the pieces. Create a loop approximately 1 in. (2.5 cm) from the previous loop and attach to a round link. Wind the remaining wire around the stem until you reach the plastic shape. Make tiny dangles with wire and beads (see page 25) and hang from the ring. Attach the earring wires. Repeat all steps for the other earring.

Egyptian eye bracelet

When I put these pieces together, it reminded me of all of the ancient Egyptian art I had seen inside the British Museum. I admired their artful skill and attention to details. It's a fun yet simple bracelet to make.

YOU WILL NEED

Basic tools

Spent (used/empty) brass bullet casing (see Helpful Hints), small coin, or vintage metal button

Vise

Dremel tool with cutting disk attachment

Safety glasses

6-in. (15-cm) length of bicycle inner tube

Small oval bezel blank

24-gauge silver wire

Link from a bicycle chain

22-gauge steel annealed wire

Silicon-based adhesive

1 Place the bullet casing in a vise and cut the top of the bullet off just below the base using the Dremel tool. Generally there is already a small groove on the bullet for the cutting tool to fit inside and begin cutting.

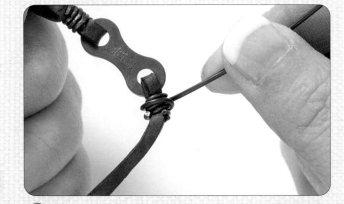

2 Cut two ⅛ in. (3 mm) wide laces from the inner tube. Thread a lace through one of the end rings on the bezel and pull round until the bezel hangs from the center of the lace. Knot the lace next to the ring then wrap with silver wire just below to secure. Thread the lace ends through the bicycle link and fold over. Wrap with 22-gauge steel annealed wire to secure. Repeat for the other side.

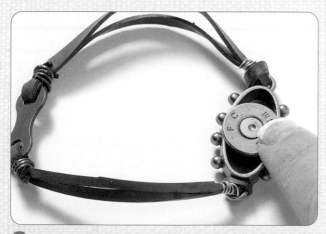

3 Glue the disk from the bullet casing into the center of the bezel. Gently pull on the cords to make sure that they are secured before wearing the bracelet.

zip it earrings

These unusual earrings are so quick and fun to make. Adjust the length by adding additional chain. Zipper pulls are also available in different sizes and colors; experiment with them to create additional looks.

YOU WILL NEED

3 in. (8 cm) of brass ball chain with two fasteners

2 brass zipper pulls

Pair of antique brass fishhook earring wires

1 Cut two lengths of ball chain each 1½ in. (4 cm) long including the fastener. Slide the first length through the top end of the zipper pull.

2 Attach the ball chain fastener to one end of the chain and complete the loop by attaching the fastener to the opposite side of the chain.

3 Add two brass jump rings to the chain, and attach the earring wire. Repeat all the steps for the second earring.

HELPFUL HINT

Recycle pulls from old zippers to get that genuine vintage look. A great place to look is on old denim jeans.

unchained melody

Combine rubber strip, bicycle chain links, and different lengths of chain to make this stylish necklace.

YOU WILL NEED

Basic tools

Bicycle inner tube

Scissors

22-gauge silver wire

2 bicycle chain links

4 square-end soda can tabs

2 eyelets

Eyelet setter

2 rivets

Rivet setter

24-gauge silver wire

36 in. (90 cm) of lightweight decorative chain

2 jump rings

12 in. (30 cm) of heavyweight double link chain

Lobster clasp

HELPFUL HINT

Placing the eyelet under the rivet stops the rivet from slipping through the hole of the soda can tab.

1 Cut a 12-in. (30-cm) length of inner tube. Fold in half and cut small slits ⅛ in. (3 mm) apart. Open out and continue cutting the slits leaving the first ¼ in. (6 mm) uncut at each end.

2 Press the end of the wire through the tube at the end. Allow one end to protrude approximately 2 in. (5 cm) and the other about ¼ in. (6 mm). Bend the ¼ in. (6 mm) end around the tube to secure in place. Insert a bike link and wrap the end of the tube around the center of the link, securing by wrapping the remaining wire end around. Trim off excess wire. Repeat at the opposite end.

3 Place two square soda can tabs together with the flat sides facing outward and set a large eyelet through one matching pair of holes as described on page 30. Repeat to make a second tab end.

4 Thread the rivet post through the chain link and the eyelet on the soda tabs. Place the back of the rivet on and set as shown on page 31.

5 Wrap the rubber cords just below each end with a short length of 24-gauge silver wire to give a finished look. Cut the lightweight chain into three equal lengths. Add a jump ring to the wire on one side and thread on the ends of the three lengths of lightweight chain; repeat on the other side.

6 Open one end of the double link chain and attach to one tab end of the necklace. Add the other end to the other tab end. Open a pair of links in the middle at the back and add the lobster clasp to one side.

disco balls

Yes, I'm a kid of the Seventies and I loved the disco era! It's a classic and these earrings remind me of the iconic disco ball. Since they are made of plastic strip they are very light and easy to wear. Color them any shade you choose to go with a favorite outfit.

YOU WILL NEED

Basic tools

Narrow plastic straw/coffee stirrer

2 × 3 in. (5 × 7.5 cm) piece of colored foil

Alcohol ink

Cotton swab

2 × 3 in. (5 × 7.5 cm) piece of clear plastic

Hole punch

2 headpins

8 size 2 mm silver beads

4 size 2 mm silver spacer beads

2 metal foil beads

2 jump rings

Pair of earring wires

1 Place the straw along the edge of the foil with the silver side facing upward and roll forward approximately three complete revolutions.

2 Cut two ½ in. (12 mm) long lengths from the straw with scissors.

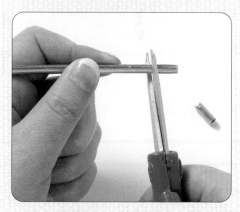

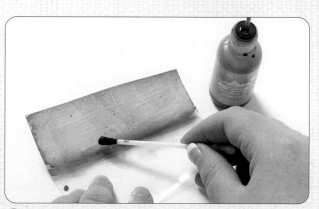

3 Color the plastic with the alcohol ink using a cotton swab.

4 Cut 12 strips from the colored plastic about ¼ in. (6 mm) wide and 1½–1¾ in. (4–4.5 cm) long. Punch a tiny hole in each end of each strip.

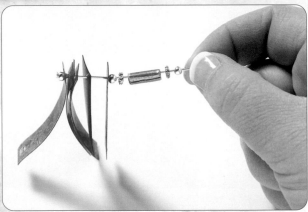

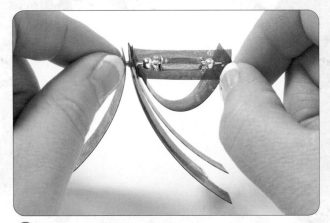

5 Thread the following in this order onto a headpin: 2 mm round silver bead, 6 plastic strips, 2 mm silver bead, spacer bead, metal foil bead, spacer bead and 2 mm silver bead.

6 Thread the other end of each plastic strip onto the headpin.

7 Press the strips downward on the headpin to form a ball, add a final 2 mm silver bead and create a loop at the top with round nose pliers. Add an earring wire with a jump ring. Repeat steps 5–6 to finish the other earring.

HELPFUL HINT

You can adapt this project to create different looks by cutting the strips from a patterned soda can or add fun patterns with paint markers.

lightning flash pendant

Use motifs and designs from soda cans as features in your designs. Here I've used the lightning flash from a popular drink can to make an interesting and bold statement necklace.

YOU WILL NEED

Basic tools

Soda can

Square of pierced metal

Ruler

Scrap paper

Double-stick sheet or tape

Hand punch

2 jump rings

Length of heavy chain

1 Cut and flatten the can as described on page 26. Measure the square of pierced metal and cut a square hole slightly smaller in a scrap of paper. Use this as a frame, moving it over the flattened can to decide on which area of the design you want to feature on the pendant.

HELPFUL HINTS

The square of pierced metal that I used as the basis of this pendant is not a jewelry finding—I found it in a hardware store. Look out for everyday materials that can be used in unconventional ways.

Although there was an available hole at the top corner of this pendant, I chose to use two holes in the middle of the top diagonal sides for a slightly different look.

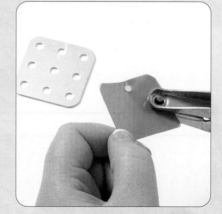

2 Cut the square from the can and add double-stick tape to the back. Place it onto the square of pierced metal and mark which holes you want to use as fixing holes. Punch the holes in the can square with a hand punch.

3 Remove the double-stick backing paper and stick the can square onto the front of the pendant. Use jump rings to attach the ends of the chain on either side of the pendant.

night owl earrings

As you begin collecting recycled materials, you'll find that just playing around with shapes and objects is quite fun. This little owl appeared doing just that. It's a neat way to add a little bit of whimsy and fun to your outfit.

YOU WILL NEED

Basic tools

4 metal buttons from old jeans

Bench block

Gold press-stud with decorative pointed ends

10 brass jump rings

2 rounded large soda can tabs

Silicon-based adhesive

Pair of earring wires

1 Hammer the back side of one metal button against a bench block so that it is flat and then repeat this with the three remaining buttons.

2 Cut off the two pointed ends from the decorative press-stud. These will be used to create the beak for each owl.

3 Add four jump rings (see page 25) to the rounded end of each soda can tab.

4 Attach the buttons with a dab of adhesive to make each owl's eyes.

5 Use a jump ring to add an earring wire to the top of each earring.

HELPFUL HINTS

Remove the rivet portion of the button from old jeans with a pair of pliers.

The little press-stud I used for the beak actually came from the hardware supply store in the picture framing section. There are all sorts of small bits of hardware you might find suitable.

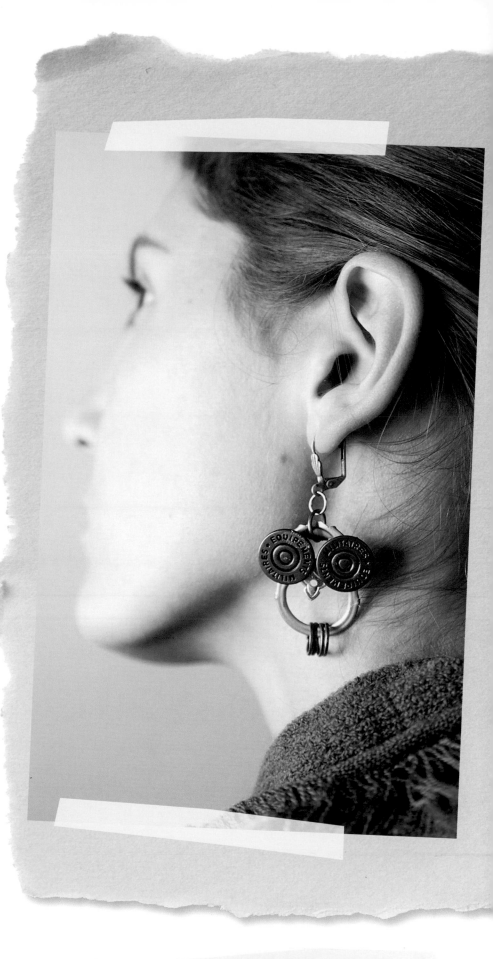

pretty polka dots

Add some zing to your life with these super bright earrings decorated with tiny glitzy polka dots. My girls at home love painting and wearing them!

YOU WILL NEED

Basic tools

Colored wire

2 soda can tabs

Nail varnish

Fine tip paint pen

Pair of earring wires

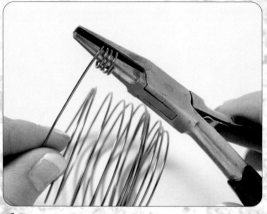

1 Create jump rings by winding a length of the colored wire around one jaw of the concave bending pliers several times and then cut off the end.

2 Slide the wire spiral off and then snip the coils into separate jump rings with wire cutters.

3 Color the soda can tabs with nail varnish on one side. Let dry and then turn over and color the other side.

HELPFUL HINTS

Making your own jump rings means that you can make them in any color, size, or shape that you want.

To add an extra sparkle, hang a drop dangle from the bottom of the tab.

4 Add tiny polka dots across the surface of both tabs with the paint pen. Let dry and then turn over and add polka dots to the other side.

5 Use a jump ring to attach a tab to the bottom of each earring wire.

biker boy keychain

You know what I love about this keychain? It's simple and it's masculine. It's hard finding things to make for our guys that will have that masculine feel. Your man will love keeping his keys on a keychain that you created especially for him!

YOU WILL NEED

Basic tools

Bicycle inner tube

D-ring

Hole punch

Grommet

Grommet setting tool

Large split ring

20 in. (50 cm) of double-link chain

Swivel trigger snap

1 Cut a 4 × 1¼ in. (10 × 3 cm) strip of bicycle tube. Fold the strip in half over the straight bar of the D-ring.

2 Punch a hole with a hole punch. Set a grommet (see page 30) through both layers about ¼ in. (6 mm) from the open end.

3 Open the end of the split ring and slide it onto the grommet.

4 Open up the links at one end of the chain, add the split ring, and close again. Repeat at the other end of the chain to add the swivel trigger clasp.

HELPFUL HINT

Cut the chain to your preferred length and, for a less chunky look, use a finer chain and a much smaller swivel trigger clasp.

lone star earrings

Conchos come in a variety of shapes and sizes and this size is perfect to create earrings with a cowgirl feel. They're so easy to whip up!

YOU WILL NEED

Basic tools

6 square-end soda can tabs

2 small rings from a bicycle chain

2 star conchos

2 washers (optional)

2 jump rings

Pair of earring wires

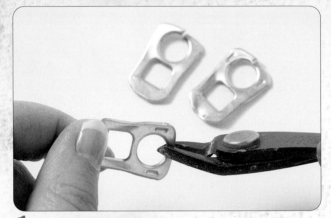

1 Snip through the top loop of each tab. Place three of the tabs together—the two outer tabs need to be flat side out.

2 Slide a ring through the cut and then line up the cut edges again neatly if necessary.

3 Check the concho against the bottom hole on the tabs and if necessary use a washer to stop the concho slipping through the hole. Unscrew the back of the concho, thread it through the bottom hole of the tab, and screw it up again from the back.

4 Use a jump ring to add an earring wire to the ring at the top of the tab. Repeat the steps to make the second earring.

HELPFUL HINT

For the top rings I used the rings left over when you dismantle a bicycle chain—you will have plenty of these left over from other projects in the book. If not, you can just substitute a jump ring.

fantastic plastic

These days credit and gift cards often come in a variety of pretty colors and with lots of cool designs and patterns. It seems such a shame to junk them when they are no longer needed. Instead, turn one into this attractive and unusual pendant and earring set.

YOU WILL NEED

Basic tools

Scrap of paper

Credit or gift card

Hole punch

Silicon-based adhesive

3 rhinestones

16 in. (40 cm) chain with clasp

Pair of earring wires

3 jump rings

1 Cut a rectangular hole the size you want your pendant to be out of a piece of scrap paper. Lay the frame onto the card and use it to identify the area you want to feature.

2 Cut out the rectangle from the credit card and round off the corners slightly.

3 Punch a small hole at the top of the rectangle.

4 Glue the rhinestone in place. For the earrings, make two smaller rectangles following steps 1 through 3. Add the large rectangle to a chain and the two smaller ones to earring wires, using the jump rings.

HELPFUL HINTS

The rhinestones I used were from a piece of broken jewelry—keep small pieces like this around to use and upcycle into your own projects.

You can make a bolder statement necklace by adding several rectangles to the chain—or for a more whimsical look, use the same concept with hearts, stars, or even circles.

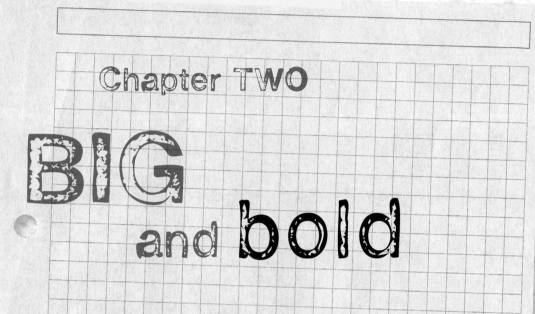

Chapter TWO

BIG and bold

Make it big, make it BOLD, and make a statement! I know whenever I'm dressed up my confidence soars and when I wear big, bold, chunky jewelry it soars even higher! Many of the projects in this chapter are unisex and can be designed or modified to appeal to the guys. Remember, you can always mix and match colors, techniques, and ideas to create designs that are uniquely you.

chunky biker bracelet

I love chunky jewelry and this bracelet is as chunky as they come! It's a great piece for both guys and gals. The rubber strip is slightly elastic and allows the bracelet to stretch so it is easy to get on, yet fits comfortably.

YOU WILL NEED

Basic tools

Bicycle inner tube

96 soda can tabs

HELPFUL HINTS

Remember to place the nice finished sides on the top and bottom of each stack.

Push the starting and finishing knots around so they are hidden inside the bracelet.

To make cutting inner tubes easy, I apply masking tape to the surface. This prevents it stretching while cutting and so keeps the strips uniform in size.

If you run out of cord in the middle, simply tie on another length and hide the knot inside the bracelet.

1 Cut lace strips about ⅛ in. (3 mm) wide from the inner tube. Taper the end of one strip, push through the hole of four stacked tabs, and knot around the end. Place the first 12 tabs together as shown in groups of four, threading the lace through the row of aligned holes.

2 Add the next stack of four tabs in the center and again thread the lace around and through the aligned holes. Add a stack of four on the top and the bottom and thread the lace to secure. Repeat these steps until you run out of tabs.

3 On one end of the bracelet you should have a set of tab stacks on either side with a single set in the middle on the opposite end. Interlock these together and thread the lace through. Knot the ends of the lace and tuck the knot inside.

ring o' roses necklace

Black is always a timeless and fashionable color. This bold necklace combines classic black with simple circle shapes to create a sophisticated statement piece.

YOU WILL NEED

Basic tools

Bicycle inner tube

Hole punch

Template on page 124

7 double-sided rivets

Rivet setting tools

Bench block

4 headpins

24-gauge silver wire

2 large silver bi-cone beads

2 jump rings

Lobster clasp

1 Cut three squares from the inner tube for each of five flowers in graded sizes. Round the squares off into circles and punch a hole through the center of each. Use the template on page 124 to cut the base piece from the inner tube and punch the holes as marked.

2 Stack a set of circles from the largest to smallest and insert a rivet through the circle stack.

3 Insert the end of the rivet through a hole on the base. Place the backing onto the rivet and then set it using the rivet setting tools (see page 30). Repeat steps 2 and 3 for the additional flowers.

4 Cut the stranded sides of the necklace as for the Unchained Melody on page 46. Wrap one end around the base of a headpin and secure by wrapping with 24-gauge silver wire. Create a large loop at the end of the headpin. Align the loop with the loop on one end of the base and set with a rivet.

5 Wrap the other end of the stranded length around another headpin and secure with wire. Thread a bead onto the end of the headpin and create a loop with concave bending pliers. Trim excess wire from the headpin. Repeat steps 4 and 5 to make the other side of the necklace. Attach a lobster clasp with jump rings.

HELPFUL HINTS

Instead of rivets you could use decorative brads with rhinestones to thread through the center of the flowers.

To create a shiny appearance to the necklace, apply a very small amount of lotion or baby oil to a paper towel and smooth onto the surface of the rubber.

coiled zipper bracelet

Metal zippers are ideal for upcycling and they look like tiny little glistening studs when seen out of context. This bracelet looks complex due to all the tiny zipper teeth details, but is actually relatively simple to make.

YOU WILL NEED

Basic tools

12 in. (30 cm) metal zipper

Square of double-stick tape sheet

Silicon-based adhesive

24-gauge silver wire

Metal finding

2 silver end cone beads

4 size 2 mm spacer beads

2 jump rings

Lobster clasp

1 Remove the zipper pull and trim the zipper close to the teeth, leaving just enough fabric to hold the teeth in place. Coil a 9-in. (22.5-cm) length of one half of the zipper tightly on a piece of double-stick sheet, adding a dab of glue under the center coil. Let the glue dry. Trim off excess tape with scissors.

2 Remove the backing from the double-stick tape. Create a zigzag with pliers in the middle of a length of wire and press onto the center of the pendant back. Glue a metal finding over the wire to finish the back of the bracelet.

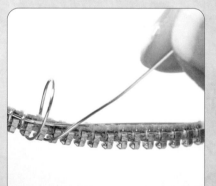

3 Cut two 6-in. (15-cm) lengths of trimmed zipper and two slightly longer lengths of wire. Lay a wire against a zipper, leaving the extra wire extending at the end on each side. Attach the wire to the zipper by wrapping an additional length of wire around and in between each tooth.

HELPFUL HINTS

Use the cut-off zipper pulls to make the earrings on page 45.

Adjust the size of your bracelet by increasing or reducing the length recommended in step 3.

4 Bend the zipper around in half and twist the wire ends together. Thread on a silver end cone bead and a round spacer. Create a loop in the wire end with concave bending pliers. Repeat steps 3 and 4 to create an additional bracelet band.

5 Thread a round spacer bead onto one end of the wire extending from the center portion of the bracelet. Form a large loop with concave bending pliers. Attach the bracelet band to this loop and then close. Repeat for the other side. Attach a lobster clasp to the band ends using jump rings.

fishing lure pendant

My Dad loves to make his own fishing lures and so has a whole box of lure-making supplies. I raided his supply to find these delicate and fun rubber tassels, which are actually the tail or skirt from a fishing jig.

YOU WILL NEED

Basic tools

40 in. (100 cm) of decorative silver chain

Eye pin

Plastic fishing lure skirt

24-gauge silver wire

Large hole (European style) silver and rhinestone spacer bead

Silver metal bead

1 large silver link

Jump ring

HELPFUL HINTS

You can find the plastic fishing lure skirt at a fishing supply store or in the sporting goods section of a department store—they come in various color combinations. If you can't find one, make a tassel similar to the one used in the tassel earrings on page 34.

My chain came complete with the little dangling arrows, but if you can't find anything similar just add some small charms to a plain chain to personalize it.

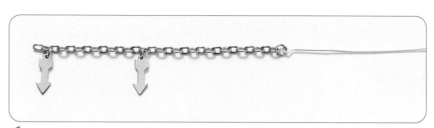

1 Cut one 4-in. (10-cm) and one 2-in. (5-cm) length of chain and attach the end of each to an eye pin.

2 Wrap the plastic fishing lure skirt around the eye pin just above the eye and secure with a short length of wire to hold it in place.

3 Slide the large hole rhinestone bead and the silver metal bead onto the eye pin assembly and push it down over the wire wrapping on the eye pin. Make a loop with concave bending pliers and remove excess wire.

4 Attach the large link to each end of the remaining length of chain. Attach the tassel to the large link with a jump ring.

loop de loop ring

I love bold and chunky and this ring is just the statement piece I like to wear. It's quite the conversation piece and no one would guess it's made from rubber!

YOU WILL NEED

Basic tools

Length of bicycle inner tube

Scissors

24-gauge wire

Rhinestone button

Silicon-based adhesive

Ring blank finding

1 Cut a 6-in. (15-cm) length from the inner tube. Cut slits into the side of the inner tube about ⅛ in. (3 mm) apart.

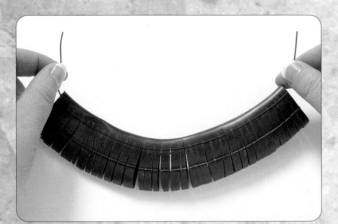

2 Thread some wire, about 9 in. (22.5 cm) long —that is, longer than the cut inner tube—through the center of the tube.

3 Holding one end of the tube and wire with pliers, wind the strip tightly around to form a circular flower. Wind the end of the wire around the coil.

4 Flatten the flower slightly on the front and glue the rhinestone button into the center, using the adhesive.

5 Attach the flower to the disk of a ring blank with adhesive.

dangle me pretty

I hope this project gets you to think of plastic drinking bottles in a whole different way. Since they are made up of transparent plastic, you'll find that they can be easily manipulated into all sorts of shapes and are easy to color as well. Use these random pieces and turn them into attractive jewelry by combining them with silver wire and a length of pretty ribbon.

YOU WILL NEED

Basic tools

Plastic drink bottle

Heat gun

Sanding block

Alcohol ink

24-gauge silver wire

16 in. (40 cm) of narrow ribbon

3 silver jump rings

2 ribbon ends

Lobster clasp

1 Cut a rough leaf shape from the plastic bottle around 2 in. (5 cm) long. Holding the shape with the pliers, heat with the heat gun until the plastic is soft and begins to curl. When you have a shape you like, allow to cool and then color with alcohol ink.

2 Wrap the shape randomly with loops of silver wire. Wrap another length of wire in loops around the center of the ribbon and attach the pendant to one of the loops with a silver jump ring.

HELPFUL HINTS

For extra interest, add some Rub'n'buff to highlight the texture of the plastic pendant after you have colored it.

I make more shapes than I think I will need so that I have a good variety to choose from. I save the remainder for future projects.

3 Slide a ribbon end onto one end of the ribbon and use the jewelry pliers to fold over the ends and set in place. Repeat this for the opposite end. Attach the lobster clasp to one end with a jump ring. Attach a jump ring only to the opposite end.

retro studded cuff

Most inner tubes are black or gray rubber, which is nice at first, but sometimes you want to add a touch of color. Painting rubber doesn't work because the paint will peel right off. A quick trip to the hardware store to get some caulking was the perfect solution and it creates amazing texture. It's an addictive technique!

YOU WILL NEED

Basic tools

Bicycle inner tube

Template on page 124

Tube of caulking

Spreader or scrap of cardstock

Plastic bag

Paint

35 small round rivets

2 larger square rivets

Black plastic tape

Hole punch

Concho

Screwdriver

1 Cut out the cuff shape from the rubber using the template on page 124. Coat the surface with caulking and stipple the surface with a crumpled plastic bag to give it texture before it dries.

2 When the caulking is completely dry, rub the paint color over the top. I like to get a little messy and use my fingers because it gives it a nicely distressed appearance.

HELPFUL HINTS

Copy the template onto paper and try it around your wrist. You can lengthen or shorten it as needed before cutting the shape from the inner tube.

Make sure to buy caulking that is paintable and clear when dry. It will go on white but will dry clear.

Rivets come in quite a variety of shapes and sizes so you can customize the look to fit your personal style.

If the rubber is thick and it's hard to get the rivet prongs through, you can make a small hole for each one first.

3 Push the prongs of a rivet through the cuff from front to back near the edge. Bend the edges of the prongs down with pliers. Add the rivets around the outer edge of the cuff. Add decorative rivets in the same way where desired.

4 Cover the back of the cuff with black plastic tape to protect your skin from the rivet prongs when wearing the cuff. Punch a hole in the middle to add the stem of the concho and screw in place from the back.

starry night lariat

This delicate and expensive-looking black-and-silver lariat is made from inexpensive black plastic drinking straws combined with glittering silver spacer beads.

YOU WILL NEED

Basic tools

Fine black plastic drinking straws

72 size 2 mm silver beads

72 size 2 mm silver spacer beads

36 silver eye pins

2 silver jump rings

1 large round silver link

1 teardrop dangle bead

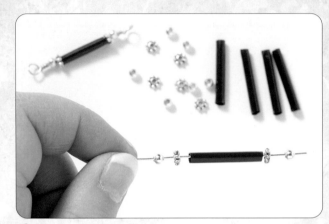

1 Cut the straws into 36 varying lengths ranging from ¾ in. (2 cm) to 1 in. (2.5 cm). Thread a silver bead, spacer bead, length of straw, spacer bead, silver bead onto an eye pin. Using concave bending pliers, curl the end of the eye pin into a loop to match the other end and then wrap the wire end around and cut off the excess.

2 Make up a second link in the same way but do not loop the end. This time thread the loop of the previous link onto the end of the eye pin first and then create a loop on the second pin and wrap the wire end as before. Repeat this step until you have added all the links.

3 Using jump rings, add the large silver link to one end of the lariat and the teardrop dangle bead to the opposite end.

HELPFUL HINT

You can make all the links individually and join them with jump rings if you prefer, but I find that making a loop and wrapping the wire end around each time is a more secure joining system.

green with envy bracelet

These tiny pieces of green, that appear to be suspended in mid-air, come together to create a delicate bracelet that is reminiscent of sea glass and the cool breeze from the ocean.

YOU WILL NEED

Basic tools

Piece of clear green plastic

Heat tool or lighter

Monofilament wire

26 crimp beads

Crimp pliers

3 jump rings

Lobster clasp

Headpin

2 size 2 mm silver beads

Small crystal bead

1 Cut small irregular squares from the green plastic. Melt the pieces of plastic slightly and shape them with pliers giving them curved edges and uneven shapes as described on page 26. Pierce a hole in the center of each piece.

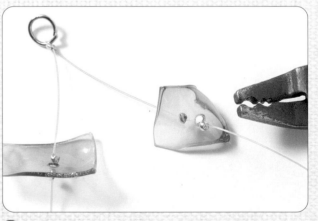

2 Cut three strands of monofilament and use a crimp bead to add the ends of all three to a jump ring, as explained on page 27. Thread a crimp bead onto one of the wires, then thread on a piece of the plastic and then another crimp bead. Position the plastic where you want it then crimp the beads on each side to hold it in place.

3 Continue adding pieces of plastic to each wire at different places. Attach a jump ring as you did in step 1 to the opposite ends of the bracelet. Attach a lobster clasp with jump rings. Use the headpin to make a dangle with the silver beads, crystal, and another piece of plastic as described on page 25. Add the dangle to the jump ring near the clasp.

HELPFUL HINTS

When adding the pieces of plastic it helps if you hang the bracelet from one end so you can see clearly where the pieces are positioned in relation to each other before you secure them.

Also try experimenting with alternative heating sources such as a candle or lighter, passing the plastic gently over the heat of the flame. You'll find each gives you a slightly different feel in the plastic and creates its own unique looks.

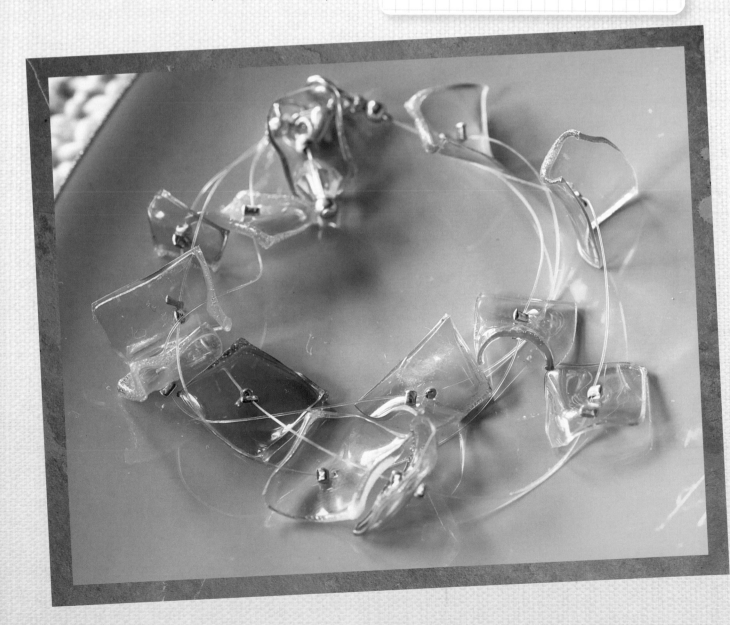

bottle cap ring

I am always collecting bottle caps that feature interesting text, color, or designs even if at that moment I don't know exactly what I am going to do with them. I wanted to create a somewhat retro design with a funky and fun vibe and this bottle cap with a star was just the one I needed.

YOU WILL NEED

Basic tools

2 metal bottle caps with interesting patterns

Silicon-based adhesive

Tiny rhinestones

Tweezers

Ring blank

1 Choose which of the two bottle caps will be the base—you won't see much of this one so the design isn't that important. Begin opening the sides out flat with the tip of the pliers.

HELPFUL HINT

Get friendly with your neighborhood restaurant as these are great sources for bottle caps and can tabs, too.

2 Place the bottle cap on a bench block face down and flatten it with a hammer. Glue the focal bottle cap to the top with adhesive and let dry.

3 Apply a tiny dot of adhesive to the back of the rhinestones. Use tweezers to set the rhinestones in place.

4 Glue the bottle cap to the ring base and allow to dry.

can-can cuff

I'm guilty! Sometimes, I buy my drinks in cans just because I like the can—this can of green tea happens to be a favorite of mine. Choose your favorite design of soda can to make this chunky cuff, which will add a touch of color and style to any outfit.

YOU WILL NEED

Basic tools

Soda can

Protective gloves

Ruler

Pen

2 large grommets

Grommet setter

7 in. (17.5 cm) of large double-link chain

Lobster clasp

2 silver jump rings

22-gauge silver wire

1 Cut a piece 2½ × 7 in. (6.5 × 17.5 cm) from the soda can (see page 26). Make a score mark down the back of the piece about ¾ in. (2 cm) in from each long edge, using the end of a pen.

2 Fold over each long side to the back along the fold lines and begin to form into the cuff shape. Don't worry—it may not stay, but just guide the aluminum along to begin forming the curve.

3 Set a grommet into each end of the bracelet as described on page 30. Open out one pair of end links on the chain and thread them through the grommet. Repeat at the other end.

4 Attach the lobster clasp to one end of the chain with a jump ring.

5 At intervals along the bracelet, punch small holes into the bracelet. Attach the chain to the cuff with wire, twisting the ends to secure and trim off excess wire.

biker chain

The double links from a bicycle chain can be used to create a chunky and masculine-looking chain.

YOU WILL NEED

Basic tools

38 bicycle chain links

Chain link tool

38 double-sided rivets

Rivet setter

22-gauge steel wire

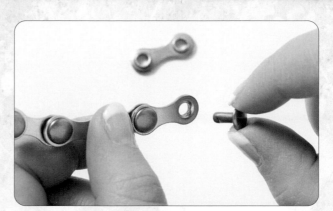

1 Dismantle the bicycle chain into individual links as described on page 31. Choose which color double links you want to use and thread the first double link onto the peg of a rivet.

2 Add a second link onto the peg and press on the rivet back.

3 Use a hammer and the rivet setter to set the rivet. Continue adding double links until your chain is the length you need.

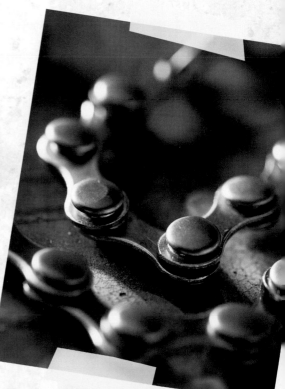

4 Cut a 3-in. (7.5-cm) length of wire and bend the top backward. Press the wire close together with pliers.

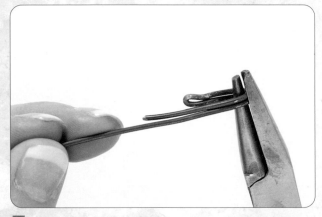

5 Use the pliers to form the doubled end into a hook.

6 Thread the single end through the last hole in the chain, and then bend the end around to form a loop. Twist the end of the wire around the loop a few times to secure.

HELPFUL HINT

When you dismantle the bicycle chain you will get two double links from each chain link, which will either be a dark gunmetal color or shiny gold or silver depending on which chain you buy. You can achieve different looks by using different links and combining them in a variety of ways.

soda fountain necklace

I thought of a fountain when I created this design. You can make this necklace as long and dramatic as you like—just keep adding more tabs until you are happy with the effect.

YOU WILL NEED

Basic tools

24-gauge silver wire

6 mm tube/rod

16 square-end soda can tabs

12 in. (30 cm) of silver chain cut in half

Toggle clasp

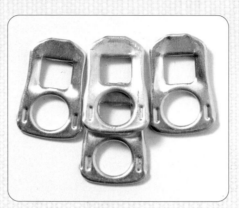

1 Using silver wire, make up 16 jump rings on the tube as described on page 56. Lay out the first four soda tabs as shown.

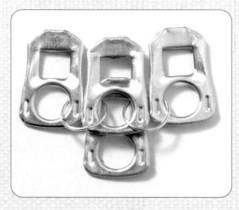

2 Join the four tabs together with two jump rings as shown.

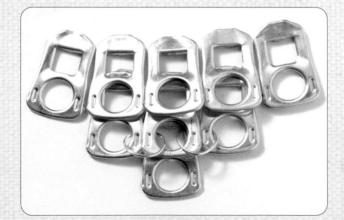

3 Add a third row of tabs in the same way, this one containing five tabs with the center three overlapping the three in the row below. These will be joined together as in the previous step, with four jump rings.

HELPFUL HINTS

It might help if you lay all the tabs out before you start joining them so you can see the structure of the necklace clearly. This will also help you to decide how long you want to make the front part of the necklace.

If you are using lightweight wire for the jump rings, solder the ends together to keep them from opening and your necklace from coming apart when you wear it.

4 The last row is seven tabs, with the center five overlapping the five in the row below, all joined together with six jump rings. Attach the chain to each side with a jump ring. Attach the toggle clasp to the opposite ends with a jump ring to complete the necklace.

Chapter THREE
handbags
and accessories

Accessories are a great way to define your personal style—
they say something about who you are and what you like.
I love accessories, because they can be easily mixed and
matched. I could have gone on and on with the ideas that
I had for this chapter alone, but here I share a few of my
favorites to inspire you.

soda tab belt

I can't even begin to imagine how many tabs I've discarded over the years—how much better to give them a grand new life. This sparkling soda tab belt is easy to make—and the more it's worn, the more flexible it becomes.

YOU WILL NEED

Basic tools
24-gauge silver wire
285 soda can tabs
Silver belt buckle

1 Cut a length of wire and wind it around the top tab to secure. Snip away the excess wire. Add the next tab with the top side up over the previous tab bottom. Wrap the wire through the hole (top of the second tab, bottom of the previous) and around again to secure both tabs together. Repeat this step adding tabs in the same way to the length of belt required.

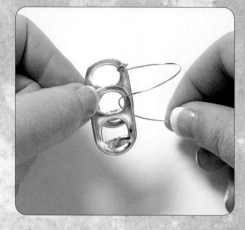

2 The second row is a repeat of the first. Begin by wrapping the wire around the top tab to secure. Add the next tab with top side up to the previous and secure the tabs with wire to the first row as shown in the picture. Continue these steps to complete three rows.

3 Wrap wire through the belt tab holes and around the buckle bar to secure the two together. Trim off any excess wire.

HELPFUL HINTS

There are two holes to each tab. The top hole of the tab is round and smooth, the bottom hole may have a sharp edge that may need to be wrapped with wire or can be bent down with pliers. I like to prep my tabs to make sure they are flat and smooth before beginning the project.

I work with manageable lengths of wire; when I run out of wire, I secure a new wire to the area where I left off.

My belt is 95 tabs per row by 3 rows. Adjust the length by adding or taking away a few rows and adjust the width by removing a row. I measure around my hips and add several inches so that the belt can overlap comfortably.

The tabs may not line up across perfectly as you first begin adding additional rows, but don't worry about it. As you add more and more tabs, the belt will become more stable.

cell phone pouch

The knitted pouch for this project was taken from a child's sweater that I purchased from a thrift store for pennies. Various sizes of child to adult sweaters can be used depending on the size of your electronic device. I love how the tabs give an updated macramé look to the pouch strap.

YOU WILL NEED

Basic tools

#18 black nylon crochet thread

22 round-end soda can tabs

2 large hole (European style) silver beads

20 large hole (European style) decorative silver beads

Sleeve from a child's knitted sweater (optional) or embellish your own case

Sewing needle and matching color thread

2 buttons

7 square-end soda can tabs

24-gauge silver wire

Decorative finding or use an old brooch

Silicon-based adhesive

HELPFUL HINT

For the pouch itself, I simply cut the sleeve off at the length desired, turned it inside out, and stitched the bottom end together. Turn right side out and fold down the top to create a cuff.

1 Cut one strand of thread 66 in. (165 cm) long and another 46 in. (115 cm) long. Fold both in half and thread the loop through the top hole of a round soda can tab. Thread the cord ends through the loop as shown.

2 Arrange the cords so that the two shorter cords are in the center. Bring the right-hand cord over the two middle cords and underneath the left-hand cord.

3 Bring the left-hand cord under the middle cords and thread it through the loop in the right hand cord. Pull on the two cords evenly to tighten the knot. This is the first half of the square knot.

4 Bring the left-hand cord over the middle cords and under the right-hand cord. Bring the right-hand cord under the middle cords and up through the loop on the right. Pull each cord on the side to tighten and complete the square knot.

5 Thread a large silver bead onto the two middle threads only, and then make another square knot underneath it. Cut the center bar on a round-end tab with wire cutters, open it up slightly and thread on a medium size bead. Close the ends of the tab back inside the bead.

HELPFUL HINTS

Because cell phones tend to be fairly small, we used a sleeve from an infant size sweater. Use the sleeve from an adult garment to make a larger pouch for an electronic tablet and then embellish with one or more of the flowers as you desire.

You can mix and match the straps from other projects in this book to give the cell phone pouch your own look. Or consider recycling a removable handle or strap from an unwanted purse or other bag.

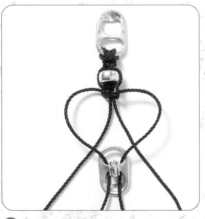

6 To attach the beaded soda tab to the cords, thread the right cord over the top of the tab, under the middle section, and back over the bottom end of the tab. Repeat this for the left side.

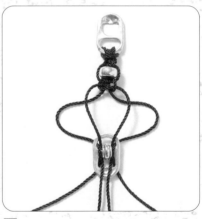

7 Thread the two middle pieces under the top tab, over the middle bar, and under the bottom end of the tab. Create another square knot following steps 3 and 4. Repeat the series of steps 4 through 7 to create the length of strap desired. Finish the strap by knotting the ends to the final un-beaded tab.

8 Sew through a button and the bottom hole of the last tab of the strap to attach the strap to either side of the pouch.

9 Arrange the seven square-end tabs into a circle and wire together through the bottom holes. Curl around and wire the first and last tabs together to create the flower.

10 Sew the flower onto the front of the pouch.

11 Glue the decorative finding into the center of the flower with a silicon-based adhesive—I used a broken brooch as my flower center.

midnight black handbag

The inspiration for this bag came from a designer handbag that cost over 400 US dollars! It was rather simple and classic in its design so I decided to make my own smart version using throwaway materials.

YOU WILL NEED

Basic tools

Large black plastic trash bag 30 gallon

Sewing machine

Masking tape

230 soda can tabs

#18 black nylon crochet thread

US size F5 (3.75 mm) crochet hook

Yarn needle and black thread

24-gauge silver wire

Black plastic tape (optional)

1 Cut the drawstring top edge off the trash bag. Fold the bag upward in half from top to bottom. With the fold at the bottom, fold over each side by ½ in. (12 mm) and sew using a ¼ in. (6 mm) seam allowance. This side will become the inside (wrong side) of the bag.

2 Fold the bag in half lengthwise again with the wrong sides out. Use masking tape to mark the side seam stitching lines—position the tape so it is slightly inward angled from the base. Stitch both sides, remove the tape and cut off the excess seam allowance. Turn the bag inside out.

3 Make a soda tab crochet strap by following the instructions on page 28. Align one end of the strap at the bottom of the seam on one side of the bag and hand stitch in place. Repeat on the other side of the bag.

HELPFUL HINTS

It can help the stability of the bag to add spray adhesive between the layers when folding the bag up in step 1.

Use a low-tack tape as a guide, otherwise it will be hard to remove the tape after sewing. If you are unable to find low-tack, you can lightly sprinkle powder onto the adhesive to reduce its tackiness. If you should sew over the tape, it can be removed from the seams, just be extra careful.

Tape the inside of the seams with black plastic electrical tape to reinforce them.

4 Secure the tabs together by wrapping with wire along the portion of the strap continuing over to the opposite side and ending where the bag begins.

soda-tab crochet purse

Don't be put off by the crochet—this project uses only single (UK double) crochet, which is really easy to learn (see page 28) and it's worth it for the fabulous result. Who would have ever thought that soda can tabs could look so stylish?

YOU WILL NEED

Basic tools

400 soda can tabs

#18 black nylon crochet thread

US size F5 (3.75 mm) crochet hook

Bulldog clip

Yarn needle and black thread

2 silver D-rings

Strip of bicycle inner tube

Ruler

Scissors

2 silver round eye swivel trigger snaps

24-gauge silver wire

Tacky glue

1 Use the pliers to squeeze each of the soda tabs flat at each end so there are no sharp edges.

2 Using the crochet thread straight off the spool, make a slip knot as shown.

HELPFUL HINTS

- -

I have found the crochet hook size given is the best for this project, but it's not critical if you have a different size, just make sure it fits though the tabs without much trouble.

Adjust the length of the strap by cutting extra length of inner tube before braiding.

This bag uses 16 rows of 25 tabs each. For a wider bag add more rows, for a taller bag add more tabs to the rows.

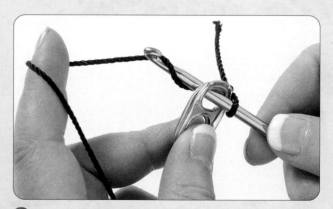

3 Place the slip knot on the crochet hook. Hold the hook in your right hand and keep the thread under tension with the fingers of your left hand. Place two soda tabs together with the flat sides facing and hold them with the finger and thumb of your left hand. Put the crochet hook through the right-hand hole in both tabs and catch the thread behind.

4 Pull the thread through so you now have two loops on your hook—the original slip knot and the new loop. Put the crochet hook over the top of both tabs and catch the thread behind. Pull the thread through both loops on the hook, so you now have one loop on the hook. You have now completed one crochet stitch. Make a second stitch through the same hole of the tabs.

5 To continue the first row, add two more tabs, one at the front and one at the back, aligning the right-hand hole over the left-hand hole of the previous two tabs and with the flat sides of both facing each other as before. Make two stitches through the aligned hole of all four tabs. Repeat this step until you have 25 tabs attached.

6 Open out the two rows just made so the flat sides are both facing up. Create a knot. Cut a long end of yarn and thread it into a yarn needle. Weave the yarn end through several stitches on the reverse and then trim off the end neatly.

7 On the following rows you only add one tab, flat side facing down, to the front of the previous row, aligning the holes. At the very beginning of the row your hook only goes through two tabs to create the first set of stitches—after that you add another overlapping tab on the same side each time, so your hook should go through four tabs to create the stitches until you come to the end of the row and then the hook will go through only two tabs again at the very end.

  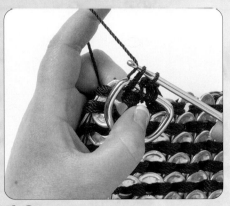

8 Complete 16 rows. Cut a long tailend of thread, thread onto the needle, and knot the ends. Secure the end on the reverse around the middle of the top edge. Fold the fabric over in half from top to bottom and align the two corners. Hold the corners in place with a bulldog clip.

9 Count nine tabs from the corner and start stitching the pair of tabs on each side of the bag together with a simple over stitch, making at least two stitches between each pair of tabs.

10 Single (UK double) crochet stitch a D-ring onto each side of the purse at the top edge.

11 Cut three strips of inner tube, each ¼ in. (6mm) wide and 18 in. (45 cm) long. Clip the three together at one end and braid the strips.

12 Thread one end of the strap through the end ring of a trigger snap, fold over and bind the two sides of the strap tightly with a length of wire. Repeat on the other side. Clip the strap onto the D-rings at the sides of the purse.

night on the town clutch

This is a great little clutch to make for an evening out. Its delicate design won't carry much weight, but it will be the perfect size to keep all your necessities together.

YOU WILL NEED

18 white plastic trash bags

Spray adhesive

Heat gun

Masking tape

Sewing machine and white thread

Foam board

Tacky glue

Silver flower finding

3 small pearl beads

1 Unfold and open out the bags. Lay one out flat on a heatproof surface and spray lightly with adhesive.

2 Add another bag on top—it doesn't need to be smooth, nicely crumpled is better. Keep adding bags until you have 8 layers. Create a second set of 8 layered bags.

3 Heat up one corner of each layered piece gently with the heat gun, taking care not to hold the heat gun too close to the plastic, so the plastic shrinks slightly and crinkles into a ruffled shape.

5 Place the two layers together and stitch along the masking tape lines. Trim away the excess along the stitching lines only, to within about ½ in. (12 mm).

4 With the ruffled point of the bag at the top, use masking tape to mark out the shape of the bag and provide a stitching line.

HELPFUL HINTS

I used small white kitchen trash bags 17 × 18 in. (42.5 × 45 cm) for this clutch bag. Vary the size of the bag to create different looks and styles.

Place masking tape over the seam if needed to provide a little extra strength.

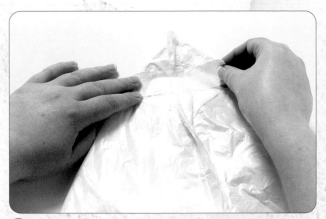

6 Remove the masking tape. Fold the bag so the side seam sits over the base seam, which will make a triangle shape at the bottom. Tape and then stitch across the base of the triangle 2 in. (5 cm) up from the tip. Repeat on the other side of the bag. This will create a gusset and flat base to allow the bag to sit flat.

7 Turn the bag right side out. To stiffen the base, cut a piece of foam board to fit, spray lightly with adhesive, and cover with another bag then insert into the bottom of the purse. Fold the front flap down and secure with glue. Fold the back flap forward and close the purse.

8 To make the flower, twist another bag to create a rope. Coil the rope into a flower shape and tack in place with glue. Attach the finding and beads to the center of the flower with glue and let dry. Attach the flower to the front of the purse with glue and let dry.

license plate purse

I'm so loving the industrial, yet fun look, to this purse! I used a vintage motorcycle license plate that I picked up for nothing at a flea market. I'm always on the lookout for things like this, which add personality to my upcycled designs.

YOU WILL NEED

Basic tools

2 vintage license plates

Tape measure

2 bicycle inner tubes

Sewing machine and black thread

Hole punch

10 large double-sided rivets

16 small double-sided rivets

Silicon-based adhesive

2 D-ring fixings

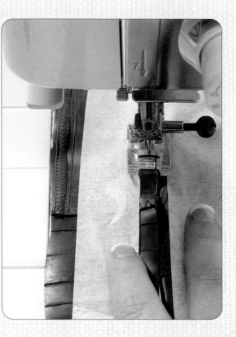

1 To make the template, measure the width of the license plate and add 1 in. (2.5 cm). Measure the depth of the license plate, add 1 in. (2.5 cm), and then double this measurement. Cut a template from paper using these dimensions. Cut lengths of inner tube, cut to open out flat, and lay them side-by-side, overlapping slightly. Zigzag stitch the pieces together over the overlapped edges using a sewing machine; this creates the initial fabric. Make sure the fabric is bigger than the template.

2 Cut out the piece for the purse using the template. Fold over with right sides together and stitch the side seams. Turn right side out. At one side fold up the corner to make a gusset.

3 Punch a hole right through all the layers and add a large double-sided rivet (see page 31) to hold the gusset in place. Repeat the steps to make a gusset on the other side.

4 Drill holes in each license plate as shown, two on top and bottom and one in the middle on the sides.

HELPFUL HINTS

Vintage U.S. license plates are available at yard sales or on eBay, so you can pick one to suit your design. Alternatively look for any suitable-size metal sign plate.

One 27-in. inner tube should be enough to make up the purse, but you will probably need a second tube for the handle—which you can make as long as you like.

Use a heavy-duty needle and increase the tension both on your needle and your bobbin when sewing the inner tubing on a sewing machine. This will help prevent your machine from locking up. Occasionally wipe the needle clean with rubbing alcohol and apply a bit of lotion or oil to the needle, this helps the needle pierce the rubber easily.

5 Place a license plate onto the purse and mark the position of all the holes to be punched out. Repeat on the reverse of the purse with the other license plate. Punch the holes in the rubber and set the rivets to hold the plates in place, a large one in each corner hole and small ones in the other four holes you just drilled.

6 Fold over the top edge of the purse and glue in place with silicon-based adhesive. Use clips to secure until dry.

7 Cut a length of inner tube as the handle. Fold the end into the D-ring fixing, mark two holes and punch the rubber. Rivet the handle to a D-ring fixing at each end using two small rivets. Rivet the D-ring fixing to the purse over the seam on each side.

boot bands

Give a pair of plain boots a touch of biker style with these rubber and metal boot bands—you can make them to any size to fit. Since they are removable, you can mix and match to create a variety of styles.

YOU WILL NEED

Tape measure

Bicycle inner tube

Scissors

Masking tape

Sewing machine and thread

Size 18 leather hole punch

Eyelet setting tool

20 eyelets

Hammer

Plastic block

Decorative hasp

8 rivets

Rivet setting tool

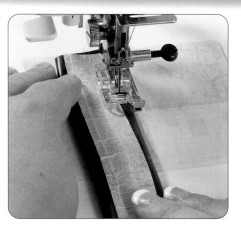

1 Measure around the boot and cut a suitable length of inner tube to match. Flatten the tube, and stitch down both sides and across the ends.

2 Mark the position of the holes for the eyelets. Place the tube on a plastic block and punch each eyelet hole out with the leather hole punch.

3 Add an eyelet to each hole as described on page 30 and set.

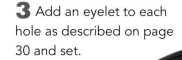

HELPFUL HINTS

Stick masking tape on either side of the inner tube to help it slide smoothly through the sewing machine. You can also add masking tape to the plate of the machine—it won't damage it and is easy to remove when you no longer need it.

Use the appropriate sized eyelet setter for the size of the eyelet you are setting, otherwise your eyelet will be crooked.

4 Slide one half of the hasp onto each end of the band and mark the fixing holes. Attach the hasp to the ends of the boot band with rivets as described on page 30. Make a second band for the other boot in the same way.

lipstick case fob

A little known fact is that I am a biker girl at heart and I used to have my own street bike. This biker chick laced rubber case can be used to carry small items of make-up, and will keep my keys organized at the same time! You could even make this in a larger size to hold a cell phone or a pair of glasses, and hang it from your belt by the split ring.

YOU WILL NEED

Basic tools

Bicycle inner tube

Size 2.8 mm punch

17 round-end soda can tabs

1 snap press-stud

Bench block

4 washers

1 square-end soda can tab

1 large split ring

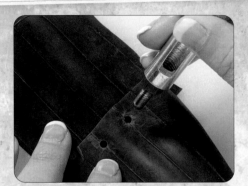

1 Cut one 4½ in. (11.5 cm) long piece and another 8 in. (20 cm) long piece from the inner tube. Overlap the shorter onto the longer by ½ in. (12 mm). Punch a hole through both thicknesses ¾ in. (2 cm) from each edge.

2 Cut four strips of inner tube each about ⅛ in. (3 mm) wide and 16 in. (40 cm) long for laces. Knot the end of one lace and bring it up through one pair of holes from underneath. Thread onto the bottom section of the soda can tab.

3 Take the lace over the side of the tab and back through the same hole. Thread the end of the lace through the other hole, back up through the tab and over the side and back through the original hole. Make a knot on the underside and clip off the excess lace. This tab will be on the back of the case.

4 Fold the longer piece over in half and punch holes at ½ in. (12 mm) intervals, approximately ¼ in. (6 mm) from the edge, through the double layers of both edges.

5 Open out the longer piece again and push the pronged half of the snap bottom through from the wrong side in the center and 2 in. (5 cm) up from the bottom edge.

6 On the right side, match the other half of the snap bottom over the prongs and press down. Hammer on the bench block to set.

7 Working from the back side of the longer piece toward the front, knot the end of the lace, thread it though a washer and through the first set of holes above the fold.

8 Thread the end of the lace through the front bottom section of a soda tab and through the next hole on the back (wrong side) pulling the end out from the front. Repeat steps 7 and 8 to work on the opposite side of the tab. Also repeat steps 7 and 8 for the other side of the case.

HELPFUL HINTS

I apply masking tape to the entire length of the tube that I am about to cut and mark the cutting lines with a pen. The tape helps keep the inner tube in place and prevents it stretching while I am cutting so that I get a nice even lace.

When lacing the sides, lace up both sides of the case at the same time to avoid having to get your hand into a small space as you work further up.

9 Add another tab and thread the lace through the front bottom of the new tab and the top of the previous tab. Insert the end through the hole in the back and then pull the end through to the front side.

10 Repeat step 9 for the opposite side of the tab and pull the laces outward to position the tab so that it is upright and straight.

11 At the top edge, loop one of the laces around to cover the edge of the tab. Knot the two laces together inside the case and cut off the excess ends. Repeat on the other side of the case.

12 Fold the flap over the main part of the case to match the position for the snap top. Set the top snap in the same way as for the bottom.

13 Round the corners of the flap with scissors. Add a square-end soda can tab over the flap snap in the same way as in steps 2–3. Make a tassel (see page 34) on the tab. Thread the split ring onto the tab on the back of the case.

inner tube belt

Custom-made leather belts can be quite expensive, but you can easily make your own custom belt using an inner tube for way less. Very easy to make and you can create your own design!

YOU WILL NEED

Basic tools

Tape measure

Bicycle inner tube

Duckbill scissors

Masking tape

Pen

Set of punches in graduated sizes

Silver lining from a potato chip/crisp bag

Sewing machine

Belt buckle

2 rivets

Rivet setter

Bench block

Belt end

Small screwdriver

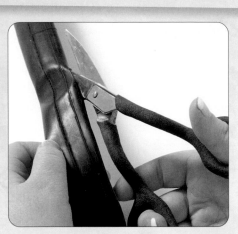

1 Measure your waist or hip area and add the extra overlap desired. Cut a length of inner tube to this measurement. Slide the thick blade of the scissors into one end and cut along one folded edge of the tube and open the tube.

2 Open out the belt flat and mark the hole placement on the masking tape. Use the set of graduated sized punches to cut the holes in the design. Repeat at 2½ in. (6.5 cm) intervals down the belt.

HELPFUL HINTS

The insides of chip/crisp bags have a variety of colored foil linings. It's so much fun to create with this foil.

You could also line the inside of the belt with patterned duck tape, keeping the tape away from the seam.

3 Cut a strip of silver bag lining to fit inside the belt between the layers so the silver shows through the holes. Stitch along each side of the belt from one end to the other.

4 Make a small hole for the prong of the buckle at one end of the belt. Slide the prong into the hole and fold the end of the belt over the buckle bar. Punch a pair of holes and use rivets, as described on page 31, to hold the end in place.

5 Cut the belt at the other end to fit the shape of the belt end. Slide the belt end onto the belt and tighten the screws to secure. Add a row of same size holes running back from the belt end to fasten the belt.

templates

These templates are provided at 100% so can be traced directly off the page.

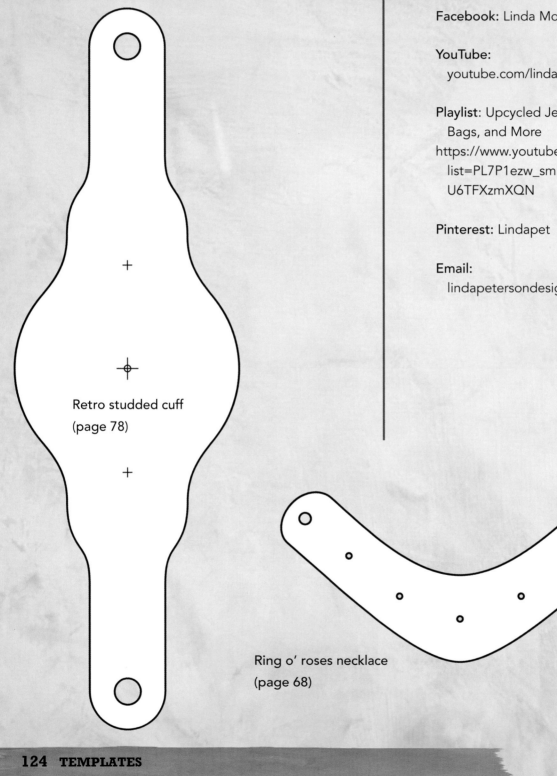

Retro studded cuff
(page 78)

Ring o' roses necklace
(page 68)

resources

LINDA PETERSON

Website: lindapetersondesigns.com

Facebook: Linda Molden Peterson

YouTube:
youtube.com/lindapetersondesigns

Playlist: Upcycled Jewelry—Belts, Bags, and More
https://www.youtube.com/playlist?list=PL7P1ezw_smi7a25H5NfxUx-U6TFXzmXQN

Pinterest: Lindapet

Email:
lindapetersondesigns@yahoo.com

US SUPPLIERS

MATERIALS
Special materials used in the projects.

MD Hobby & Craft
Teflon gloves, duckbill scissors
www.mdhobbyandcraft.com

Fiskars
Scissors
www.fiskars.com

Walmart
Bicycle chain, inner tube
www.walmart.com

Beadalon, Inc
Basic jewelry findings, jewelry
making tools, small hand tools
www.beadalon.com

Ranger Inc
Inks, color wash
www.rangerink.com

Amaco., Inc.
Rub-N-Buff®
www.amaco.com

GENERAL CRAFT
Craft materials and tools.

Hobby Lobby Stores
www.hobbylobby.com

Michaels Stores
1-800-642-4235
www.michaels.com

A.C. Moore
1-888-226-6673
www.acmoore.com

Jo-Ann Crafts
1-888-739-4120
www.joann.com

HARDWARE SUPPLIERS
Specialty nuts, bolts, chains, and pipe.

Ace Hardware
www.acehardware.com

Lowe's Inc.
www.lowes.com

The Home Depot
www.homedepot.com

UK SUPPLIERS

MATERIALS
Materials used in the projects.

Amazon
Teflon gloves, duckbill scissors,
scissors, Rub-N-Buff®
www.amazon.co.uk

Halfords
Bicycle chain, inner tube
www.halfords.com

The Bead Shop
Basic jewelry findings, beads,
charms, jewelry making tools
www.the-beadshop.co.uk

GENERAL CRAFT
Craft materials and tools.

Hobbycraft
Stores nationwide
0800 0272387
www.hobbycraft.co.uk

Crafty Devils
Online store
www.craftydevilspapercraft.co.uk

John Lewis
Stores nationwide
www.johnlewis.com

The Craft Barn
Online store
www.thecraftbarn.co.uk

The Range
Stores across England and
online store
www.therange.co.uk

HARDWARE SUPPLIERS
Specialty nuts, bolts, chains, and pipes.

B&Q
Stores nationwide
www.diy.com

Homebase
Stores nationwide
www.homebase.co.uk

The publishers would like to thank Janome for loaning the sewing machine used in the sewing steps.
www.janome.co.uk

index

acknowledgments

Just as they say it takes a town to raise a child, it takes a great team to create a book! While I may be the name on the front cover, this book is not possible without the help of my great team—my publisher, Cindy Richards and her talented team of Sally and Carmel; my personal editor, Marie Clayton, who spent endless hours poring over my words; my photographer, Geoff Dann, who is brilliant at making my work shine, and his assistant, Marc Harvey and to my project stylist, Luis Peral-Aranda and style photographer, Emma Mitchell. Thank you all for each of your talents and efforts into creating this book! You are the best!

Also a great big shout out to the best hand-model ever, my daughter Mariah Welsh for her patience and help in creating this book. I couldn't have done it without her!

To my family, my ever supporting husband, Dana, and kids—thank you for jumping in and getting things done while I poured my soul into this book. This is a sacrifice of love from you to me. I love you all!